Learning about Cats

THE BIRMAN CAT

by Joanne Mattern

Consultant:
Eugene A. Boroff
Past Birman Breed Council Secretary
Cat Fanciers' Association

CAPSTONE
HIGH-INTEREST
BOOKS

an imprint of Capstone Press
Mankato, Minnesota

Capstone High-Interest Books are published by Capstone Press
151 Good Counsel Drive, P.O. Box 669, Mankato, Minnesota 56002
http://www.capstone-press.com

Library of Congress Cataloging-in-Publication Data
Mattern, Joanne, 1963–
The Birman cat/by Joanne Mattern.
    p.cm.—(Learning about cats)
    Includes bibliographical references (p. 45) and index (p. 48).
    ISBN 0-7368-0895-7
    1. Birman cat—Juvenile literature. [1. Birman cat. 2. Cats. 3. Pets.] I. Title.
II. Series.
SF449.B5 M37 2002
636.8'3—dc21   00-013071

Possum Grape
15.95   3/02

Summary: Discusses the history, development, habits, and care of Birman cats.

Editorial Credits
Leah K. Pockrandt, editor; Lois Wallentine, product planning editor; Linda Clavel,
    cover designer and illustrator; Katy Kudela, photo researcher

Photo Credits
Carl J. Widmer, 4, 10
Chanan Photography, 18
Cheryl A. Ertelt 9, 16, 24, 27, 28, 31, 32, 35, 39
Eugene Boroff, 36
Mark McCullough, cover, 6, 20, 40–41
www.ronkimballstock.com, 13, 15, 22

1 2 3 4 5 6 07 06 05 04 03 02

Table of Contents

Quick Facts about the Birman 4

Chapter 1   The Birman Cat 7

Chapter 2   Development of the Breed . . . 11

Chapter 3   Today's Birman 17

Chapter 4   Owning a Birman 23

Chapter 5   Caring for a Birman 29

Photo Diagram 40

Quick Facts about Cats 42

Words to Know 44

To Learn More 45

Useful Addresses 46

Internet Sites 47

Index 48

Quick Facts about the Birman

Description

Size: Birman cats have long, stocky bodies. They are medium-sized cats.

Weight: Males weigh between 10 and 14 pounds (4.5 to 6.4 kilograms). Females are slightly smaller. They weigh between 7 and 11 pounds (3.2 and 5 kilograms).

Physical features: Birmans have long, muscular bodies. Their long, thick fur is soft to the touch.

They have wide, round heads. The shape of their blue eyes is nearly round.

Color: Birmans have light-colored coats. The fur on their ears, face, paws, and tail is darker than their coats. These dark areas of fur are called points.

Development
Place of origin: Birman cats are thought to be from the country of Burma. This southeast Asian country now is called Myanmar.

History of breed: It is believed that Birman cats originated from a pair of Birman cats sent to France in 1919. The breed became popular in Europe. The cats especially were popular in France and England. The first Birman cats came to the United States in 1959.

Numbers: In 2000, the Cat Fanciers' Association (CFA) registered 998 Birmans. Owners who register their Birmans register the cats' breeding records with an official organization. The CFA is the world's largest organization of cat breeders.

Chapter 1

The Birman Cat

The Birman cat breed's popularity is increasing in North America. Many people like Birmans because they are playful, calm, and affectionate. People also value the breed's long fur and color markings.

Appearance

A Birman is a medium-sized cat. Males can weigh as much as 14 pounds (6.4 kilograms). Females can weigh as much as 11 pounds (5 kilograms). A Birman cat's long body is sturdy and muscular.

Birmans are longhaired cats. Their fur is thick and soft. But their fur does not mat like the fur of many other longhaired cat breeds.

One of the breed's most noticeable features is white markings called gloves and laces. Gloves

Many people value the Birman's long, thick coat and varied color markings.

are markings on the cats' paws. Laces are the markings on the cats' back legs.

Birmans have an unusual color pattern. They have long, light-colored coats with colorpoints. Colorpoints are the dark areas of fur on Birmans' ears, tails, faces, and legs.

Birman cats have four common coat colors. These colors are seal point, blue point, chocolate point, and lilac point. Seal-point Birmans have ivory coats with dark brown points. The point color on some seal-point Birmans is so dark that it almost looks black. Chocolate-point Birmans have ivory coats with light brown points. Blue-point Birmans have blue-white coats with dark blue-gray points. Lilac-point Birmans have off-white coats with light pink-gray points. The ideal Birman coat color has a slight golden tone. But the coat color may look different depending on the point color.

Birman kittens are born white. Their points begin to appear when they are a few days old. Birmans may be 1 year old before their permanent markings fully develop.

Personality
Birmans are friendly cats. They seem to enjoy being around people and other animals. Birmans' gentle personalities make them good pets for

Birmans have markings called laces on their back legs.

families. Birmans also get along well with dogs and most other cats. Birman cats do not seem to like to be alone. Owners should have other pets in the house if no people are at home during the day.

Birman cats usually are very calm and quiet. They seldom meow. Birmans sometimes are playful. But they seem to prefer to lie quietly and watch the activities of people and other animals. Because of these actions, many people describe the Birman as a polite cat.

Chapter 2

Development of the Breed

The Birman name comes from "Birmanie." This word is the French spelling for Burma. The Birman often is called "the Sacred Cat of Burma." The Birman got this nickname because some people believe that the cats lived in temples with priests.

A Holy Legend

No clear record of the Birman's origin exists. But there is one popular story that describes the legend of the Birman cat. A priest named Mun-Ha lived in the Temple of the LaoTsun. People worshiped a blue-eyed goddess named Tsun-Kyan-Kse at this temple. Mun-Ha was the temple's head priest. He lived at the temple with his white cat named Sihn.

The Birman cat often is called "the Sacred Cat of Burma."

11

One day, thieves attacked the temple. They killed Mun-Ha in front of a golden statue of Tsun-Kyan-Kse. Sihn placed his feet on his master and faced the golden statue. Sihn's white fur then took on a golden glow. His face, ears, legs, and tail turned dark brown to match the earth. But Sihn's paws turned white where they touched his master's head. This change represented purity. His eyes also turned from yellow to dark blue.

The legend says that Mun-Ha's soul left his body and entered Sihn. The cat stayed by his dead master's body for seven days before he also died. Some people believed Sihn carried Mun-Ha's soul up to heaven when he died. After Sihn's death, the coat and eye color of the other 99 cats in the temple also changed. The legend says that each cat carries the soul of a priest on his final journey to heaven. This legend is why the Birman is known as "the Sacred Cat of Burma."

The Birman in Europe

The origin of the first Birman cats in Europe is as mysterious as the origin of the breed. No one is really sure when the first Birman cats came to Europe. One story says that two Englishmen

A legend tells how Birmans received their coloring.

helped Burmese priests protect their temple during World War I (1914–1918). The men were Major Gordon Russell and August Pavie. To show their thanks, the priests later sent a pair of Birmans to the men. At that time, Russell and Pavie lived in France. Another story says that a wealthy American named Vanderbilt received a pair of cats from a temple servant while in Burma. The story then says that Vanderbilt sent the cats to a friend in France named Thadde Hadisch.

It is known that someone in Burma sent a pair of Birman cats to another person in France in 1919. The male Birman was named Maldapour. The female cat was named Sita. Maldapour did not survive the long journey. But Sita gave birth to a litter of kittens when she arrived in France. One kitten was named Poupee. Many people believe that Poupee was bred to a Siamese cat. This breed has markings similar to those of a Birman. In 1925, French cat associations recognized Birmans.

The breed almost died out in Europe during World War II (1939–1945). Only two Birmans were alive at the end of the war. These cats were bred to Persians and cats of other breeds. This outcrossing allowed the Birman traits to continue.

Birmans in America

The first Birman cats probably arrived in the United States in 1959. In 1961, a breeder named Gertrude Griswold received two seal-point cats as a gift. She later discovered that these cats were Birmans. She arranged to breed her Birmans with Birmans from France. One of

Birmans were outcrossed to Persians to preserve the breed's features.

Griswold's cats was the father of the Cat Fanciers' Association's (CFA) first Birman grand champion. This cat's name was Griswold's Roman of Bybee.

Other North American breeders imported Birmans from England and France. Today, the Birman cat is an important breed in North America. But the breed still is more common in Europe.

Chapter 3

Today's Birman

Many people think of the Birman as an ideal companion. The breed is not as active as some shorthaired breeds or as inactive as some longhaired breeds. Many people appreciate the Birman's appearance and affectionate personality.

Colors and Patterns

The original point colors of Birmans are seal, blue, chocolate, and lilac. These colors are called traditional Birman colors because they all naturally occurred in the breed. Breeders later outcrossed Birmans to cats of other breeds. This outcrossing produced Birmans of different colors.

Today's Birmans can be a variety of colors and patterns. Lynx points have lightly striped coats and heavily striped points. Tortie points or tortoiseshells have points that resemble tortoise shells. These points are brown mixed with blue,

One of the new Birman patterns is lynx tortie point.

Lilac-point Birmans have light-colored points.

lilac, or light and dark red. These colors also are mixed with shades of light and dark cream. Breeders sometimes breed cats with these basic colors and patterns to produce cats with several other color patterns.

Birman Points
All Birman cats have points. The colorpoints are produced by a special gene in Birman cats. Genes are parts of cells that are passed from parents to

their offspring. Genes determine how the offspring will look.

This special gene is heat sensitive. Cool parts of the Birman body have dark fur. These body parts include the ears, tail, face, and paws. Warm parts of the Birman body have lighter-colored fur. All animals with this gene are born with white coats. Dark-colored Birmans develop their colors earlier than light-colored Birmans do. Dark-colored Birmans such as seal points may begin to develop their color a few days after birth. Light-colored Birmans such as lilac points may take a few more days to develop their color.

The Birmans' gloves and laces should look a certain way for competition. The gloves should stretch across each paw in an even line. The laces should end in a point on the back of the cats' legs. The gloves and laces appear sooner on dark-colored Birmans than on light-colored Birmans. It may take several weeks for the gloves and laces to appear on light-colored Birmans. It is rare for a Birman to have four perfect white gloves.

Birmans' coat and coloring are important parts of the breed standard.

Breed Standard

The Birman's popularity is increasing in North America. Many Birman cat owners enter their cats in shows. Judges look for certain physical features when they judge Birmans in cat shows. These features are called the breed standard.

The general breed standard says that Birmans should have long, stocky bodies. Birmans' thick legs should not be too long in relation to their body. The paws should be round. A Birman cat's head should be wide and round. The cheeks should be very round. The ears should be medium-sized and set wide apart. Their eyes must be blue and almost round. The Birman's bushy tail should be of medium length.

The coat is an important part of the Birman breed standard. Birmans' coats should be long, thick, and soft. The light-colored body fur should strongly contrast the dark fur of the points.

Naming a Birman

Most U.S. Birman breeders follow a French tradition of naming their cats. This tradition is to give all kittens born in the same year names that begin with the same letter. For example, all kittens born in 2000 received names that began with the letter "X." All kittens born in 2001 received names that began with the letter "Y."

The naming system renews every 26 years. No letters of the alphabet are skipped. In 2003, the naming system will start with the letter "A." This system also makes it easy to tell the age of a Birman cat.

Chapter 4

Owning a Birman

People can adopt Birman cats in several ways. They may contact animal shelters, rescue organizations, or breeders.

Animal Shelters

Many people adopt cats from animal shelters. These places keep unwanted animals and try to find homes for them.

People consider adopting a cat from an animal shelter for several reasons. Many people believe they are saving cats' lives. Shelters often have more animals than there are people available to adopt them. Cats that are not adopted often are euthanized. Shelter workers euthanize cats by injecting them with substances that stop their breathing or heartbeat. Shelters also offer less expensive pets than breeders. Breeders often

People who want a show-quality Birman should contact a breeder.

People can find excellent pets from animal shelters and breed rescue organizations.

charge several hundred dollars for a Birman. Most shelters charge only a small adoption fee. Veterinarians often provide discounts on medical services for adopted shelter cats.

People who want to adopt a purebred Birman may want to avoid shelters. Shelters often have mixed-breed pets available. People interested in adopting a Birman should have patience. They can ask shelter workers to contact them if a Birman is brought to the shelter. It may take several months for a shelter to receive a purebred Birman.

Shelter cats often have unknown histories. Shelter workers have little or no information about the animals' health, parents, or behavior. This lack of information could lead people to adopt cats with medical or behavioral problems.

But many good pets are available at animal shelters. A shelter adoption is a good choice for people who do not plan to breed or show their Birman cats. Shelter cats usually do not have papers showing that they are registered with an official cat organization. Owners who do not have papers for their cats can exhibit them only in the household pets group at cat shows.

Breed Rescue Organizations

People interested in adopting a purebred Birman can contact a breed rescue organization. Organization members find homes for unwanted or neglected cats.

Breed rescue organizations are similar to animal shelters in many ways. But these organizations specialize in certain breeds of cats or dogs. They seldom euthanize the animals. Rescue organizations keep Birmans until they find homes for them.

Adopting a Birman from a breed rescue organization also may have some advantages over shelters or breeders. Rescue organizations only charge small fees for adopting cats. These cats even may be registered.

People can locate Birman rescue organizations in several ways. These organizations often have their own Internet sites. They sometimes advertise in magazines or newspapers. Animal shelters also may refer people to Birman breed rescue organizations.

Birman Breeders

People who want to adopt show-quality or good pet-quality Birman cats should buy one from a good breeder. Good breeders carefully select their cats for breeding. They make sure that the cats are healthy and meet the breed standard. Breeders usually own one or both of the parents of the kittens they sell. Owners can meet the kittens' parents. This opportunity gives new owners an idea of how the kittens will look and behave as adults.

Many Birman breeders sell retired cats that were used for breeding. Breeders usually retire cats after three to five years of breeding. These cats cost much less than Birman kittens. Good breeders usually have their female cats bred once each year. It can be unhealthy for cats to have kittens more often than once each year.

Good Birman breeders never use Birmans with health problems for breeding.

People can find Birman cat breeders in several ways. People can attend cat shows to talk to Birman breeders and see their cats. Breeders also advertise in magazines and newspapers. Some breeders have Internet sites. People should get the medical histories of the breeders' cats before they buy a cat. They also should check the breeders' references. People can contact others who have bought cats from the breeders. These owners can provide information about their experiences with the breeders.

Chapter 5

Caring for a Birman

Birmans are strong cats. With good care, Birmans can live long lives. It is common for a healthy Birman cat to live 15 or more years.

Dental Care

Birman cats need regular dental care to protect their teeth and gums from plaque. This coating of bacteria and saliva causes tooth decay and gum disease. Dry cat food helps remove plaque from cats' teeth. But owners also should brush their Birmans' teeth at least once each week. Owners can use a soft cloth or a toothbrush and toothpaste made for cats. Owners should never brush a cat's teeth with toothpaste made for people. Cats may become sick if they swallow it.

As Birmans age, they may need more than regular brushing. They may need to have a veterinarian clean their teeth once each year.

Birmans need their teeth brushed regularly.

Grooming

Birmans' coats are easier to care for than other longhaired cat breeds. Owners should brush their cats' coats at least once each week. A natural bristle brush is best to use. Synthetic or plastic brushes often create static electricity. Electricity builds up in the Birmans' fur when owners brush them. Owners can use a comb on thick areas of the coat. Owners should brush their Birmans more often during spring. Cats shed their heavy winter coats during this season. Frequent brushing will help get rid of loose hair.

Owners must gently brush or comb their Birmans. Brushing or combing too hard breaks off pieces of fur. Owners also can scrape their cats' skin if they brush or comb too hard.

Most cats do not need baths. But Birmans' long coats should be bathed every one to three months. Owners should use a shampoo made for cats. Most cats resist getting wet. It is best to start bathing Birmans when they are kittens. The cats then become used to being bathed.

Nail Care

Birman cats need their nails trimmed every few weeks. The tip of a cat's claw is called the nail. Regular trims help to reduce damage if Birmans

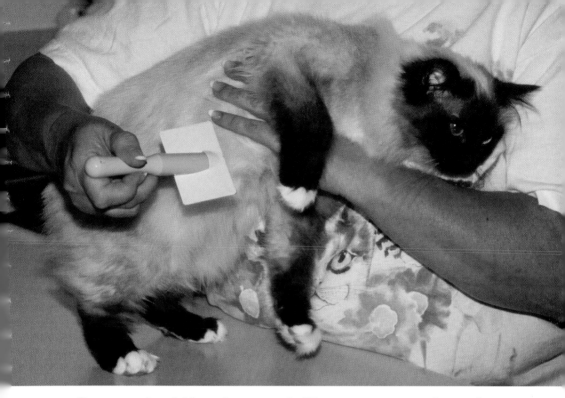

Owners should brush or comb Birmans once each week.

scratch carpet or furniture. Nail trimming also
protects Birmans from infections caused by
ingrown nails. Infections can occur when a cat
does not sharpen its claws often. The claws then
grow into the bottom of the paw. Nail trimming
also prevents Birmans from other paw injuries
such as snagging their nails on carpet.

Owners should start trimming their Birmans'
nails when the cats are young. Kittens will
become used to having their nails trimmed as
they grow older. Veterinarians can show owners

Birmans use scratching posts to sharpen their claws.

how to trim their cats' nails with a special
nail clipper.

Indoor and Outdoor Cats

Some cat owners allow their cats to roam
outdoors. This practice is not safe. Outdoor cats
are at much greater risk for disease than cats that

are kept indoors. Cats that roam outdoors also face dangers from cars and other animals.

Indoor cats need a litter box. Owners fill the box with small bits of clay called litter. Cats eliminate waste in litter boxes. Owners should clean the waste out of the litter box each day. They should change the litter often. Cats are clean animals. They may refuse to use a dirty litter box.

Both indoor and outdoor cats need to scratch. Cats mark their territories by leaving their scent on objects that they scratch. Cats also scratch to release tension and keep their claws sharp. This habit can be a problem if cats scratch on furniture, carpet, or curtains. Owners should provide their cats with scratching posts. People can buy scratching posts at pet stores or make them from wood and carpet or sisal rope. This strong rope is made from plant fibers.

Veterinarian Visits

Birman cats need regular veterinary visits. Most veterinarians recommend yearly checkups for cats. Older cats may need to visit a veterinarian two or three times each year. Older cats tend to have more health problems than younger cats. Veterinarians can better treat these problems if they see the cat more than once each year.

Owners who adopt a Birman should schedule a checkup appointment as soon as possible. The veterinarian will check the cat's heart, lungs, internal organs, eyes, ears, mouth, and coat.

The veterinarian will give vaccinations to the Birman. These shots of medicine help prevent serious diseases such as rabies and feline panleukopenia. Rabies is spread by animal bites and can be deadly. Most states and provinces have laws that require owners to vaccinate their cats against rabies. Feline panleukopenia also is called feline distemper. This virus causes fever, vomiting, and death. Cats also can be vaccinated against respiratory diseases. These diseases include the rhinostracheitis virus, calici virus, and chlamydia psittaci.

Some owners vaccinate their cats against feline leukemia. These owners allow their cats to roam outside or board their cats in kennels. Feline leukemia attacks a cat's immune system. It leaves the cat unable to fight off infections and other illnesses. Feline leukemia is spread from cat to cat by bodily fluids.

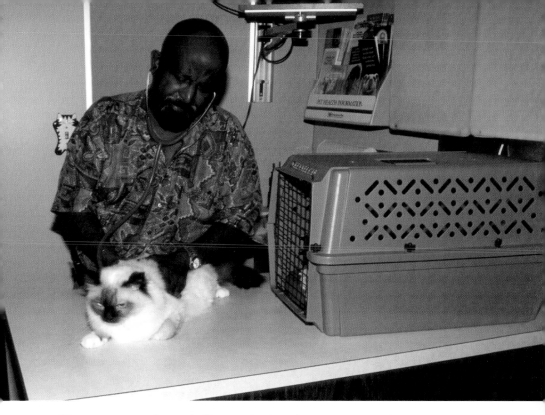

Birmans need to visit a veterinarian once each year.

Cats should receive some vaccinations each year. They receive other vaccinations less often. Breeders and veterinarians have information on which vaccinations Birman cats need. Owners should keep a record of their cats' vaccination dates. This record helps owners be sure that their cats have received all the needed vaccinations.

Veterinarians also spay female cats and neuter male cats. These surgeries make it impossible

Breeders can provide new owners with the medical histories of their kittens.

for cats to breed. Owners who are not planning to breed their cats should have them spayed or neutered. These surgeries keep unwanted kittens from being born. They also help prevent diseases such as infections and cancers of the reproductive organs. Spayed and neutered cats usually have calmer personalities than cats that are not spayed or neutered. They also are less likely to wander away from home to find mates.

Health Problems

Birman cats have few health problems. The most common problem is hairballs. Many longhaired cats have hairballs at some time in their lives. Cats swallow loose pieces of fur when they clean themselves. This fur can form into a ball in the cat's stomach. The cat then needs to vomit the hairball. But large hairballs can become trapped in a cat's digestive system. A veterinarian may have to perform an operation to remove these hairballs.

Regular brushing and bathing are the best ways to prevent hairballs in Birmans. Brushing and bathing removes loose fur before cats can swallow it. Birman owners also can give their cats medicines to treat hairballs. These medicines contain petroleum jelly. The jelly forms a coating on the hairballs in the cat's stomach. It helps the hairballs pass harmlessly in the cat's waste.

Cats sometimes inherit diseases from their parents. Good cat breeders test their animals for these diseases. They will not breed animals that suffer from serious illnesses. Breeders should provide owners with information on their cats' medical histories. This information is important to new owners when choosing a Birman cat.

Feeding

Birman cats need high-quality food. Many pet foods available in supermarkets or pet stores provide a balanced, healthy diet. Veterinarians and breeders also can give owners advice about what type of foods to choose.

Some owners feed their Birmans dry food. This food has several advantages. It usually is less expensive than other types of food. Dry food can help keep cats' teeth clean. It also will not spoil if it is left in a dish.

Other owners prefer to feed their Birmans moist, canned food. This type of food should not be left out for more than one hour or it may spoil. Owners who feed their cats moist food usually feed their adult cats twice a day. The amount of food needed depends on the individual cat.

Both dry and moist foods are suitable for Birman cats. Owners can offer their cats both types of food to see which type the cats prefer.

Some Birmans prefer to eat moist cat food.

Cats need to drink plenty of water to stay healthy. Birmans should have fresh, clean water to drink at all times.

Cat owners need to provide their pets with proper nutrition, grooming, and regular veterinary visits. Owners who follow these basic guidelines can help their Birman cats live long, healthy lives.

Whiskers

Ears

Points

Chest

Paws

Gloves

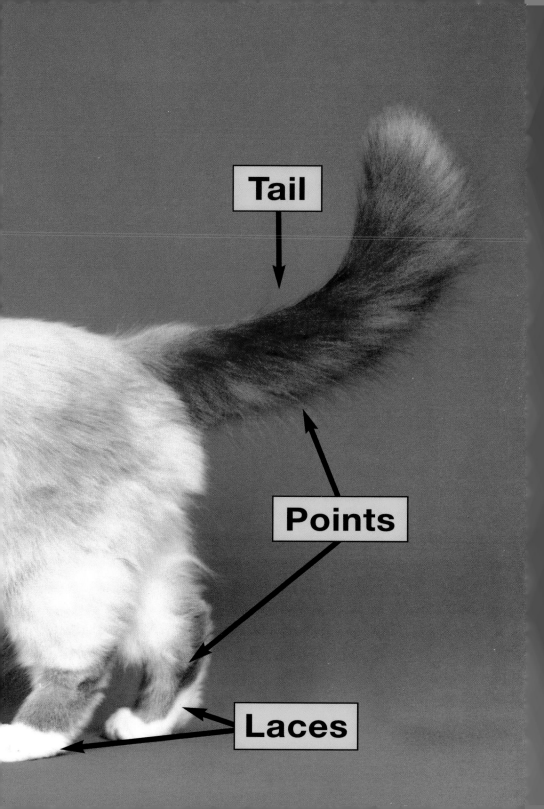

Tail

Points

Laces

Quick Facts about Cats

A male cat is called a tom. A female cat is called a queen. A young cat is called a kitten. A family of kittens born at one time is called a litter.

Origin: Shorthaired cat breeds descended from a type of African wildcat called *Felis lybica*. Longhaired breeds may have descended from Asian wildcats. People domesticated or tamed these breeds as early as 1500 B.C.

Types: The Cat Fanciers' Association accepts 40 domestic cat breeds for competition. The smallest breeds weigh about 5 to 7 pounds (2.3 to 3.2 kilograms) when grown. The largest breeds can weigh more than 18 pounds (8.2 kilograms). Cat breeds may be either shorthaired or longhaired. Cats' coats can be a variety of colors. These colors include many shades of white, black, gray, brown, and red.

Reproduction: Most cats are sexually mature at 5 or 6 months. A sexually mature female cat goes into estrus several times each year. Estrus also is called "heat." During this time, she can mate with a male. Kittens are born about 65 days after breeding. An average litter includes four kittens.

Development: Kittens are born blind and deaf. Their eyes open about 10 days after birth. Their hearing develops at the same time. They can live on their own when they are 6 weeks old.

Life span: With good care, cats can live 15 or more years.

Sight: A cat's eyesight is adapted for hunting. Cats are good judges of distance. They see movement more easily than detail. Cats also have excellent night vision.

Hearing: Cats can hear sounds that are too high for humans to hear. A cat can turn its ears to focus on different sounds.

Smell: A cat has an excellent sense of smell. Cats use scents to establish their territories. Cats scratch or rub the sides of their faces against objects. These actions release a scent from glands between their toes or in their skin.

Taste: Cats cannot taste as many foods as people can. For example, cats are not very sensitive to sweet tastes.

Touch: Cats' whiskers are sensitive to touch. Cats use their whiskers to touch objects and sense changes in their surroundings.

Balance: Cats have an excellent sense of balance. They use their tails to help keep their balance. Cats can walk on narrow objects without falling. They usually can right themselves and land on their feet during falls from short distances.

Communication: Cats use many sounds to communicate with people and other animals. They may meow when hungry or hiss when afraid. Cats also purr. Scientists do not know exactly what causes cats to make this sound. Cats often purr when they are relaxed. But they also may purr when they are sick or in pain.

Words to Know

breeder (BREED-ur)—someone who breeds and raises cats or other animals

breed standard (BREED STAN-durd)—certain physical features in a breed that judges look for at a cat show

estrus (ESS-truss)—a physical state of a female cat during which she will mate with a male cat; estrus also is known as "heat."

euthanize (YOO-thuh-nize)—to painlessly put an animal to death by injecting it with a substance that stops its breathing or heartbeat

neuter (NOO-tur)—to remove a male animal's testicles so that it cannot reproduce

points (POINTZ)—dark-colored areas of fur often found on Birman cats' ears, faces, legs, and tails

spay (SPAY)—to remove a female animal's uterus and ovaries so that it cannot reproduce

vaccination (vak-suh-NAY-shun)—a shot of medicine that protects a person or animal from disease

To Learn More

Commings, Karen. *Guide to Owning a Birman.* Popular Cat Library. Philadelphia: Chelsea House, 1999.

Cutts, Paddy. *Cats: A Comprehensive Guide to the World's Breeds.* San Diego, Thunder Bay Press, 1998.

Maggitti, Phil. *Birman Cats: Everything about Acquisition, Care, Nutrition, Breeding, Health Care, and Behavior.* A Complete Pet Owner's Manual. Hauppauge, N.Y.: Barron's, 1996.

Petras, Kathryn, and Ross Petras. *Cats: 47 Favorite Breeds, Appearance, History, Personality, and Lore.* Fandex Family Field Guides. New York: Workman Publishing, 1997.

You can read articles about Birman cats in *Cat Fancy* and *Cats* magazines.

Useful Addresses

Canadian Cat Association (CCA)
289 Rutherford Road South
Unit 18
Brampton, ON L6W 3R9
Canada

Cat Fanciers' Association (CFA)
P.O. Box 1005
Manasquan, NJ 08736-0805

The International Cat Association (TICA)
P.O. Box 2684
Harlingen, TX 78551

The National Birman Fanciers
P.O. Box 1830
Stephenville, TX 76401

Sacred Cat of Burma Fanciers, Inc.
4329 East Airport Road
Mount Pleasant, MI 48858

Internet Sites

**American Veterinary Medical Association
   Presents: Care for Pets**
http://www.avma.org/care4pets

Animal Network
http://www.animalnetwork.com

Birman Home Page
http://www.birman.org

Canadian Cat Association (CCA)
http://www.cca-afc.com

Cat Fanciers' Association (CFA)
http://www.cfainc.org

The National Birman Fanciers
http://www.vcnet.com/valkat/nbf/nbfenter.html

Sacred Cat of Burma Fanciers
http://www.scbf.com

Index

animal shelters, 23, 25, 26

breeder, 14, 15, 17, 18,
    21, 23, 25, 26–27, 35,
    37, 38
breed rescue organization,
    25–26
breed standard, 20–21
Burma, 11, 12, 13, 14

coat, 8, 12, 17, 19, 21,
    30, 34

dental care, 29

Europe, 12, 14, 15

food, 29, 38
France, 13, 14, 15

gloves, 7–8, 19
Griswold, Gertrude, 14–15
grooming, 30, 39

Hadisch, Thadde, 13

litter box, 33

Maldapour, 14
Mun-Ha, 11, 12

Pavie, August, 13
Persians, 14
personality, 8–9, 17
points, 8, 17–18, 19, 21
Poupee, 14

Russell, Major Gordon, 13

"the Sacred Cat of
    Burma", 11, 12
scratching posts, 33
Siamese cat, 14
Sihn, 11, 12
Sita, 14

Tsun-Kyan-Kse, 11, 12

United States, 14

vaccinations, 34, 35
Vanderbilt, 13